M000282675

A MAN
with a **RAKE**

©2022 Ted Kooser

ISBN 978-1-7349791-7-6

Published by Pulley Press, an imprint of
Clyde Hill Publishing

Cover and book design by Dan D Shafer

Cover and title page illustration by Ted Kooser

The back-cover photograph is of an antique hay pulley
owned by the author.

ACKNOWLEDGEMENTS

Some of these poems were previously published:
"Up Early Writing" in *Poetry East*; "From a Low Hill"
in *American Journal of Poetry*; "A Glint" in *Hudson Review*;
"A Mouse Nest" in *Rewilding*, an anthology edited by Crystal
Gibbins; "On High Ground" in *Nimrod*; "A Fox" in *New Ohio
Review*. "A Man with a Rake" was posted on Facebook.

Thanks to my wife, Kathleen Rutledge, for her help in
selecting the poems.

A MAN
with a RAKE

Poems by **TED KOOSER**

**PULLEY
PRESS**

Shod with wings is the horse of him who
rides on a Spring day
the road that leads to home

PO CHÜ-I
as translated by Arthur Waley

THE POEMS

GUMBO

The ghosts of the old German farmers
are up early today, drinking coffee,
standing at their kitchen windows
thinking that soon the last drifts of snow
in the lee of the windbreaks will melt
and be gone, and their fields will be just
dry enough to be turned, and they can
follow March into April, placing their
four-buckle galoshes into the prints
of their horses, feeling happy and free
though not letting it show. But today
they're just standing there, looking out,
framed in the broken black windows
of dead houses, bales stacked in the rooms,
a quarter mile back from the road,
the earth turning the earth on its own.

UP EARLY, WRITING

My very old dog licks and licks
at a spot on the carpet, his mouth
making the hollow, rhythmic sound
of water gurgling out of a jug.
There can be nothing to taste there
but dust, or perhaps it's the smell
of an earlier, more interesting self.
For almost an hour, I too have been
trying to summon a complicated,
spooned-and-stirred-together smell,
that of my great-aunt Annie's kitchen
on a wet spring day in the forties,
with a burlap bag of new potatoes
slumped by the door, a Mason jar
of bacon grease pushed to the back
of the cooling range, and my sweaty
but freshly-aproned great-aunt Annie
with a soggy, sagging cardboard box
of squealing piglets, hastily pushed
with a dirty bare ankle under the table,
snorting and tossing their straw.

FROM A LOW HILL

From a low hill, looking out and down,
mid-June, mid-day, the corn already
in the ear and heavy, leaning out into
the rows, and this for miles and miles
on either side, under a burning sun,
what little blue there was bleached
from the heavens, no breeze at all,
and nothing moving through all this
but a tiny runner half a mile away,
padding along a gravel road between
these two great sides to everything,
as if in the fold between two pages
of an enormous ledger, a him or her
raising little puffs of dust so far away
that it's hard to tell if whoever it is
may be coming or going, a figure
hopping about on a spot of shadow
which, after you stop to watch a while,
appears to be going away, so that
in a few more minutes there may be
nothing moving throughout all this
vista, the dusty, sun-flattened colors
like those in a Japanese woodblock,
no minuscule, faraway villager
down in one corner, a straw hat
obscuring his face, leading a donkey
laden with bundles of cornstalks
up a long trail into the always.

A GLINT

I watched a glint of morning sunlight
climbing a thread of spider's silk
in a gentle breeze. It shinnied up
from the tip of a dewy stalk of grass
to an overhanging branch, then
disappeared into the leaves. But soon
another followed, and then another,
glint after glint, and though they made
no sound, what I could see was music,
not melody but one clear, shining note
plucked over and over, as if the sun
were tuning the day, then handing it
to me so I could be the one to play it.

FARM SALE

Arriving late, a man in his sixties
has parked at the end of a long line
of pickups pulled off on the shoulder.
He's got a long walk to the gate,
climbing down out of his truck
and adjusting his ball cap, then
slamming the door, though so far
down the road that we can scarcely
hear the thunk. And now he's
starting uphill out of what must be
a near silence, little more than
a whisper of breeze in the fence
and the red cedars behind it,
walking up into the auctioneer's
amplified prattle. The blue June sky
is reflected in each pickup's windows.
So is he. Even from this far off
you can see that he's liking the look
of himself as he passes. He's got
his cap on square, nothing better
to do on a warm Saturday morning
than to park at the far end of
where all of the others have parked,
and to walk up the road, in no hurry
to see what's for sale at the sale.

SHELTERBELT

From a mile off, it's a coarse, knotty seam
clumsily stitched from odd snippets of thread,
black, gray and green, but somehow it's holding,

suspending the heavy brown corduroy fields
from the thin cotton sky, nothing you'd want to
show off in Home Ec class, but finding a use,

makeshift curtain, hung there since the thirties,
pieced from scrap fabric, using native trees,
cedar and ash, and tacked over a window

with a whispery, all-season crack at the far
back of the present, in an unheated room
used for storing the dusty old past.

BULL

Stopped on a shoulder I watched a great bull
closed in by a gate. He was traveling alone
with no luggage but the two thousand pounds
piled on his shoulders. Before him grazed
maybe three dozen cows with rumps turned
to him as they fed, and he called out
with a bellow that began at the tip of his tail
and roared forward, scouring him out
like a bottle-brush, so that at its last note,
the little black tuft on his belly drooped
damply, and the grand sound of his yearning
fell away frail in the distance, having
flown through those cows like a butterfly
without even so much as a lick. But then came
another great bottomless holler, and another
only a few feet behind. They were like
hiccups, but worse, far more painful to hear.
Whatever it was that was pumping him dry
had no mercy. And the cows? They'd turned
deaf ears, with blue or red or yellow tags,
and I rolled up my window to shut out
his terrible pleading, turned up the radio,
and blithely drove on toward Des Moines.

A MOUSE NEST

It had been built in my band saw, inside the steel housing,
two halves like a shirt box on end, with a lid to unfasten,
exposing the pulleys and blade, a perilous place for a nest,
a couple of fistfuls of yellow fiberglass insulation
brought from afar, wad by wad, and neatly packed into
the spokes of a pulley that hadn't been spun for a while,
although now I was hoping to use it, to cut out a fiberboard
seat for a chair that a two-year-old visitor had climbed on,
putting a foot through the caning. I suspected there might
be a nest: there were fiberglass tufts that had fallen out onto
the saw's metal table. So, before switching it on, I unfastened
the housing to look. There was the nest, exposed to the light,
big as a softball, split and flattened to fit that tight space,
and dirty, too, like cotton candy somebody had dropped
on a midway. It all looked unoccupied, nobody at home,
my whole workshop now holding its breath, then it stirred,
and out pushed the whiskery nose and shiny black eyes
of a mouse, which then, face to face with its tormentor
drew back in that innocent fiberglass cloud with no sign
of a storm building inside. I picked up a wood shim
that lay handy, and stealthily started to pick away pieces.
At first there was no sign of life, but as I worked in toward
the center I sensed pandemonium building, the kind
you'd see when a storm-warning siren far in the distance
starts insisting a tornado's coming, and suddenly that
mother mouse bolted for safety, four mouselets aboard,
hanging onto her nipples, all of them slipping and sliding
down the back side of the housing, tumbling out on the floor,

scrabbling for purchase, the whole load dragging into
the shadows beyond, but for one who had either let go
or pulled loose and fallen away: a mouse in miniature,
about the size of a brazil nut, with sleek gray fur and ears
too small to hear much, eyes so tiny or so tightly closed
I couldn't see them, nor, I supposed, could they see me.
I left it where it fell and picked out the rest of the nest,
which was pissy and warm at its middle, put back the saw's
housing—a housing indeed!—and cut out the chair seat
while beneath me, between my enormous brown shoes
the mouse feebly kicked with its back feet, trying to push
the overturned boat of itself under the edge of a toolbox,
the thin oars of its forelegs stretching to pat at the floor,
and when I had finished my work I turned out the light
and left it there in its predicament, adrift on a sea
of despair no bigger than a jar lid. Hours later, before
going to bed, I walked down to my workshop to look,
and snapped on the overhead light, and entered the stillness,
where every trace of what had happened to us there
was gone, except for a little red fiberboard sawdust.

A MAN WITH A RAKE

Under his faded, soft, fisherman's hat
and lifting his face to the early spring sun,
he's stopped for a moment to rest, up to
his ankles in leaves he's drawn into
the center of a circle of green. He's propped
some of his weight on the rake, the end
of its handle locked in a knot of his fingers
and this pressed to a cheek, his eyes closed.
Before this he'd been watching the rake
tick around clockwise, minute to minute,
a fine afternoon passing forever away,
but he's figured out now how to slow it
all down, both hands clasped on the end
of the second-hand, holding it back.

WALKING OUT FOR THE MAIL

A mailbox across the highway from a house
set back in trees down a long gravel lane
and a woman in overalls, sweater and scarf
on the shoulder, waiting for traffic to pass.

Not one of us has the least place in her life,
not a chair in her kitchen, nor a window
to peer from, parting a curtain, nor an old pair
of boots to pull on to walk out for the mail.

Wind from the cars and trucks tugs at her scarf
as she waits, cupping her elbows, squinting
east and then west, all the way out to the
vanishing point, not meeting our eyes as we pass.

THE CLOSED ROAD

Sandburs, cockleburs, wild roses and switch grass
have nearly erased the closed road, though the gravel
resists, packed hard, an aggregate of color,
pebbles of yellow and red, white chips of quartz
still finding a little warmth among the shadows.
And to either side, along ditches where rain ran,
filling the beer cans and bottles with sand,
gray cedar fence posts stand or lean, or help
each other stand or lean, though most of them
have already fallen, all clutching the same rusty wire,
tugging them out of one season and into the next.

A SEPIA PHOTOGRAPH

Light brushes coats of brown varnish
over the past, lets each coat dry
for a generation before adding another.

Who were these two people, the man
standing just to her side, his hand
on her shoulder? They've ridden up

to the front of this oval of walnut
and glass on an uncomfortable bench
like those on a Ferris wheel, with

younger couples out of sight but
swinging down and in behind,
and they've rocked to a stop, the man

stepping off and now waiting for her,
while she gathers her skirts and tries to
recall where she set down her smile.

A PUMP IN A FIELD

It's often the last thing left standing
after the farmhouse, barn, and outbuildings
have been bulldozed, piled and burned
and the ground's been plowed over for corn,
a pump on a concrete, card-table-sized slab
with its handle removed as if to discourage
some stranger from stopping to draw up
a drink. A person who unbolts a handle
and drives it away in the back of a pickup
puts us on notice, not only that the water
is theirs but that its music, too, is theirs
to listen to, should they choose to come back
with the handle, and fit it on, and pump it
and pump it and pump it, up to the surface,
those squeals with the cold bell-like clanks
far below, then the beautiful gurgle.

ON HIGH GROUND

Back in those days the hardships often came
down stream—high water in spring, hog cholera,
mud and manure from a neighbor's cows,
a pawed-up run of sand in the long dry years
of the nineteen-thirties. A man in his eighties
told me one day over lunch that his parents
and grandparents, and he and his brother
and two young sisters, had been camped one night
out of the wind in a prairie hollow, sleeping
under their wagons, and a heavy rainstorm
miles upstream sent down a six foot wall of water
that rushed into their camp. Their father carried
the two little boys to a rise, ran back for his wife
and the others, but his wife, his two young girls,
and his in-laws were gone, swept into the night
still rolled in their canvas tarps. I've observed
in the light of that story how the places we sleep
climb higher and higher over the generations,
the first house dug out of a hill and roofed
with sod, close to the water, then it's a shack
yards higher up the slope—tarpaper and slats
with a hand-dug well—then a two-story house
perched right on top, sided with clapboards,
with windows on all four sides and one of them
in a room at the back of the second floor
for watching far upstream, into the nightfall,
to see in advance the big troubles to come.

BANKSIDE

There was a part of the river that kept to itself,
that was slow, forever idling along in the shade
of the trees on the bank, turning and turning,

now and then having picked up, upstream,
the wand of a willow branch, lazily drawing
big circles that overlapped, like a chain, not like

the heavy steel chain you might think of, but one
pasted together out of loops of brown paper,
a kindergarten chain. Now and then it came past

with a bottle it found, or pushing a log along,
but that kind of thing was never a chore for it,
just summer idleness. That was the part I loved,

that *I'm-off-by-myself-but-enjoying-it* side
of the river that I'd call Hello to, that warm part
I reached for, putting my hand on its shoulder.

A FOX

For Dan Gerber

I saw a red fox stepping in and out
of the shadows of tall granite stones
in a cemetery's oldest section, fur
flaring as she entered each patch
of sun, though her feet and the tip
of her tail were too darkened by dew
to be set alight. She was quite small
but in her presence the stones forgot
their names. Above her the canopy
was respectfully opening oak by oak
to light her way, though she offered
no sign that she expected any less.
I couldn't move for fear she'd stop
and fix me with those eyes that had
already stopped everything there,
the headstones, the plastic flowers,
I, too, now breathless as I watched
her pass along that long, long hall,
a flame reflected in its many doors.

INK BLACK

It was a very bright day, and for miles,
August had burned off all the color.
Here and there I could see a farmstead,
lifted just slightly above the surface,
like the head of a nail working up out
of a shingle. Back from the road sat a gray,
plank-sided shed with a sheet-metal roof
held in place by the smoldering sun.

The fourth wall was open to the south,
and if ever there was an "ink black" this
was it: anything taken inside had sunk
from sight as in a pail of crankcase oil.
All the black in the county was there,
dragged up, rolled in, shoved to the back,
then more heaped up in front, the last bits
pitched on the top to settle in layers dense
as coal. If you needed a bucket of black
or a length of darkness, this was the place
to find it, free. Every shadow for miles
was making a bee-line right for that hole.

But then I saw a little faint light from
a crack between two of the boards
and all the black I'd seen, and thought
I'd felt, that I'd even imagined I could
hear—a creaking and clatter, the squeal

of old machinery, a century or more
of utter blackness I could almost taste,
like oily metal shavings—all of that
packed to the rafters, bowing the walls,
was, as my eyes adjusted, very slowly
leaking away, that shed too flimsy
to hold it all, and I could then make out
a thin gray absence waiting there,
which had an altogether different story.

MOON SHADOWS

All night the moon was a lamp held steady
while an oak, alone on the crusted snow,
composed a long letter, thoughtfully forming
each word in the copperplate script
of its shadows. From a window halfway up
the stairs I watched it at work, the pale blue
airmail stationery smoothed and waiting
and the sentiments coming so slowly
that I grew impatient and climbed up to bed.
And I fell asleep wondering to whom
the tree might have been writing, and why,
and when I awoke the sky was gray
and cold, the sun hidden in clouds,
and the tree was just standing there,
reaching up into a few scattered snowflakes
then beginning to fall, not trying to catch them,
but letting them slip through its branches,
and the letter, whatever its message, was gone.

TED KOOSER lives and writes on 62 acres of wooded hills and pasture in rural Nebraska with his wife, Kathleen Rutledge, a retired editor of the *Lincoln Journal Star*. None of their property is farmed and is instead left to an abundance of wildlife. For many years Kooser worked at a desk in the life insurance business, retired at 60, and for fifteen years taught poetry writing in the graduate program of the University of Nebraska. He is the author of fifteen books of poetry, five volumes of nonfiction, five children's picture books, and seventeen chapbooks and special editions. He served two terms as U.S. Poet Laureate and his 2004 collection of poems, *Delights & Shadows*, was awarded the Pulitzer Prize. Prior to the publication of *A Man with a Rake*, his most recent collection of poems is *Red Stilts*, from Copper Canyon Press. More about his life, his work, and his many honors can be found at www.tedkooser.net.

CPSIA information can be obtained
at www.ICGtesting.com
Printed in the USA
LVHW010058070322
712739LV00008B/396

9 781734 979176